Can You Guess What I Am?

In the Rainforest

JP Percy

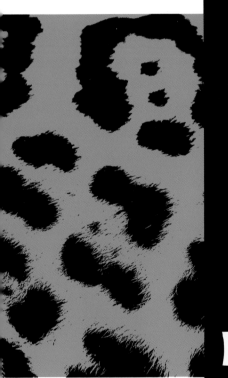

W
FRANKLIN WATTS
LONDON·SYDNEY

How to use this book

A **tropical** rainforest is a hot, wet place where lots of trees and other plants grow very close together. Tropical rainforests have rain almost every day. Many types of plants and animals live in a rainforest **habitat**.

This book combines the fun of a guessing game with some simple information about things found in a tropical rainforest.

Start by guessing
- Carefully study the picture on the right-hand page.
- Decide what you think it might be, using both the picture and the clue.
- Turn the page and find out if you are right.

Don't stop there
- Read the extra information about the animal or object on the following page.
- Turn the page back – did you miss some interesting details?
- Have a go at the fun activities on page 22.

Enjoy guessing and learning
- Don't worry if your guess is wrong – this happens to everyone sometimes.
- Your guessing will get better the more you learn.

Words in **bold** can be found in the glossary on page 23.

I am a tree!

Rainforest trees can grow more than 60 metres tall. They have deep roots, which stop them falling over.

Under the canopy the rainforest is a dark place. Trees have to grow tall to reach the sunlight.

I am an ant!

In rainforests, there are more ants than any other type of insect.

Ants are very strong for their size. Some can carry more than 50 times their body weight. A trap-jaw ant can crush its prey with its super-strong jaws.

I am a colourful **reptile** with a long, sticky tongue to catch prey, such as ants. Can you guess what I am?

I am a
chameleon!
(ka-MEE-lee-on)

Chameleons live on trees.
They use their toes – and
sometimes their curly tails –
to grip tree branches.

Panther chameleons come in
lots of different colours, such as
red and blue. Some chameleons
can change the colour of their
skin. They do this if they are
excited or scared.

I am a flower!

Orchids (*OR–kids*) are plants that live on rainforest trees. Their flowers come in lots of beautiful colours.

Orchid roots do not grow in soil like other plants' roots. Instead, they grow into the branches or trunk of the tree they live on.

I have damp skin and my young are called tadpoles.

I am a frog!

Poison dart frogs live on the ground and on rainforest trees – not in ponds. They have special toes to help them climb.

Poison dart frogs have poison on their skin. The patterns and colours on their skin tell other animals to stay away!

I am a toucan!

Toucans are rainforest birds. They can't fly very well. Instead they hop and glide from branch to branch.

A toucan's bill can be nearly half as long as its body. They use their bills to pick and peel the fruits they eat.

We are Monkeys!

Squirrel monkeys use their tails to help them balance on branches, so they don't fall off!

Some monkeys can use their tails like an extra hand. This helps them move among rainforest trees. It is safer for monkeys to stay in the canopy, far away from large **predators**.

I am a jaguar!

Jaguars are big cats with spotted fur. They have whiskers, just like a pet cat.

Jaguars are predators. They hide among the plants so they can quietly creep up on their prey, such as monkeys and birds.

I am full of water and I twist and turn through the trees.

I am a river!

Many rainforests
grow around huge rivers.

The water helps plants grow and animals live.
People live in rainforests too. They use the
rivers to move from place to place.

The Amazon is the most famous rainforest river.
It is the second-longest river in the world!

Now try this...

Draw it!

Poison dart frogs come in lots of crazy colours. Ask an adult to draw or download some simple frog outlines. Use a picture (or your imagination) to colour in your frog's skin to match the names of these poison dart frogs:

- strawberry poison dart frog
- bumblebee poison dart frog
- spotted poison dart frog

(note: these are all real kinds of poison dart frog!)

See it!

You can see the animals in this book at many zoos and safari parks. Use this book to write a list of animals. Take it with you and tick off all the aniamls you spot if you are lucky enough to visit. What other rainforest animals could you add to your list? Here are a few to get you started:

- parrot • tree snake
- tarantula spider
- spider monkey
- sloth • fruit bat

Match it!

The rainforest is one of many different habitats around the world. Match each animal below to the habitat it lives in.

jaguar	ocean
camel	**Arctic**
whale	river
polar bear	rainforest
penguin	grassland
crocodile	forest
bear	**Antarctic**
giraffe	desert

(answers on page 23)

Glossary

Antarctic the very cold and icy land and seas around the South Pole.

Arctic the very cold and icy area around the North Pole.

canopy the treetops in a rainforest forest, which form a layer of branches and leaves.

habitat the natural home of a plant or animal.

insect a small animal with six legs and usually one or two pairs of wings.

poison a substance that can kill or make people or animals sick.

predators animals that eat other animals.

prey animals that are eaten by other animals.

reptile a cold-blooded animal that has a backbone and dry, scaly skin.

roots the part of a plant, usually underground, that holds the plant firmly so it won't fall over. Roots suck up water so the plant can make food.

tropical the areas of the world just above and below the Equator. (The Equator is an imaginary line around the centre of the Earth.)

Index

Match it! answers
The correct habitat for each animal is:
• jaguar = rainforest • camel = desert • whale = ocean • polar bear = Arctic • penguin = Antarctic • crocodile = river • bear = forest • giraffe = grassland

Franklin Watts
First published in Great Britain in 2016 by The Watts Publishing Group

Series editor: Amy Stephenson
Art director: Peter Scoulding
Picture Credits: John Anderson/Dreamstime: 18. Edurivero/Dreamstime: 14.
happykamill/Shutterstock: front cover tr, 9. David Havel/Shutterstock: front cover br, 7, 8.
Gabriela Insuratelu/Shutterstock: 10. Kguzel/Dreamstime: front cover bl, 13.
Lightpoet/Dreamstime: 15. Johnny Lye/Shutterstock: 19, 20-21.
Mgkuijpers/Dreamstime: front cover tl, 11, 12. Orionmystery/Dreamstime: 5, 6.
Subin Pumsom/Dreamstime: front cover tr, cl, cr, bc; 17. Dr Moreley Read/Shutterstock: 3, 4.
Marzanna Syncerz/Dreamstime: 2, 22. Jordan Tan/Dreamstime: 16.

Dewey number: 333.75
ISBN: 978 1 4451 4473 3
Library eBook ISBN: 978 1 4451 4477 1

Printed in China

Franklin Watts
An imprint of
Hachette Children's Group
Part of The Watts Publishing Group
Carmelite House
50 Victoria Embankment
London EC4Y 0DZ

an Hachette UK company.
www.hachette.co.uk

www.franklinwatts.co.uk